BRITAIN IN OLD P   S

AROUND HAYES & WEST DRAYTON

A SECOND SELECTION

EDITED BY
PHILIP SHERWOOD

SUTTON PUBLISHING LIMITED

Sutton Publishing Limited
Phoenix Mill · Thrupp · Stroud
Gloucestershire · GL5 2BU

First published 1998

British Library Cataloguing in Publication Data
A catalogue record for this book is available from the
British Library.

ISBN 0-7509-1649-4

Typeset in 10/12 Perpetua.
Typesetting and origination by
Sutton Publishing Limited.
Printed in Great Britain by
Ebenezer Baylis, Worcester.

Philip Sherwood was born in Sipson but now lives in Harlington where, on his mother's side, his family has lived for many generations. He was educated at Bishopshalt Grammar School and later at Birkbeck College of the University of London where he obtained a degree in Chemistry. He is a chemist by profession and is a Fellow of the Royal Society of Chemistry. As a Principal Scientific Officer in the Scientific Civil Service he has worked at the Transport (formerly Road) Research Laboratory and the Royal Commission on Environmental Pollution, but now works as a self-employed consultant.

He has written many articles and books on the local history of the Harmondsworth/ Harlington area including the first selection of *Around Hayes & West Drayton in Old Photographs*, *Heathrow and District in Times Past*, *More About Heathrow and District in Times Past*, *The History of Heathrow*, *Heathrow and District Past and Present* and *The Villages of Harmondsworth*. He also lectures extensively. He has been the Treasurer of the Hayes & Harlington Local History Society for many years and is also the Hillingdon area representative for the London Branch of the Council for the Protection of Rural England.

CONTENTS

Heathrow Airport under construction, 1946. Viewed from the south-west, the Perry Oaks sludge works are in the foreground. It would have been impossible to achieve the civil airport without a lengthy public inquiry which the Air Ministry would almost certainly have lost. To get round the problem the Ministry pretended the airfield was urgently needed by the RAF which allowed it to use the Defence of the Realm Act to requisition the land illegally in the alleged pursuit of the war. Work started in May 1944, only six weeks before D-Day and, as the photograph shows, work had not proceeded very far by the time the war ended. The runway lying diagonally across the photograph was known to be entirely unsuitable for civil aviation but had to be built to keep up the pretence that it was to be a military airfield. It cost £350,000 to build at 1945 prices and was rarely used. The development of the airport completely changed the character of the area covered by this book. (Photograph courtesy of the RAF Museum, Reference No. 6082–9)

INTRODUCTION

This book, like the first volume published in 1996, contains old photographs of the area which until 1965 came under the administration of the former Urban Districts of Hayes and Harlington and of Yiewsley and West Drayton. These, for better or worse (mostly worse), now form the southern part of the London Borough of Hillingdon but to some extent still retain their own identities as the former Middlesex villages from which they are descended. Because of this historical background the book is divided into separate sections dealing respectively with Hayes, Harlington, Yiewsley, West Drayton and the four villages of the parish of Harmondsworth (Harmondsworth, Longford, Sipson and Heathrow).

The earliest photograph in this collection dates from 1866 but the majority cover the period 1920 to 1960. Some more recent photographs have also been included because the rate of change in the area covered by the book is such that even pictures taken only five years ago assume historical interest. At times it is easy to imagine that within this area there is a determined effort to eradicate all traces of the past. Indeed the very existence of Harlington, Sipson and Harmondsworth is continually under threat from the expansion of Heathrow which, like a cancerous growth, threatens to destroy the whole area. It is therefore important to put on record what the locality looked like even quite recently.

Books of old photographs are often condemned by professional historians as being self-indulgent exercises in nostalgia. But if older people, whether or not they still live locally, find pleasure in recalling the appearance of the area in which they grew up, why should they not? However, this is not by any means the only purpose of this book, nor of its predecessor. Many people living in the locality are not aware of its past and a society with no such recollections is unlikely to have either cohesion or much interest in its present. A knowledge of local history can make seemingly dull streets and mediocre buildings come to life. People who are ignorant about the past of where they live are missing much that could improve their quality of life and give them a greater sense of identity with the local community.

It must be admitted that many of the buildings shown in the photographs, and which have since disappeared, had little architectural or historical significance. Nevertheless their inclusion, with their associated street scenes and former local industries, is a reminder of a totally different way of life which is well within living memory. For people residing in some of the old buildings shown in the photographs, their demolition and replacement by modern developments must have resulted in an improvement in standards of living. We cannot, nor should we wish, to prevent this but when all that can be said in favour of change is taken into account, the fact remains that many old buildings of historical and local importance have been quite needlessly, even wantonly, destroyed. By putting this on record we can but hope that a more enlightened attitude will be taken to the historical buildings that remain and that they will be preserved for posterity. In the words of William Morris (1834–96), 'It has been most truly said that these old buildings do not belong to us, only that they belonged to our forefathers and they will belong to our descendants unless we play them false. They are not in any sense our property to do what we like with them. We are only trustees for those who come after us.'

P.T. Sherwood
Harlington, 1998

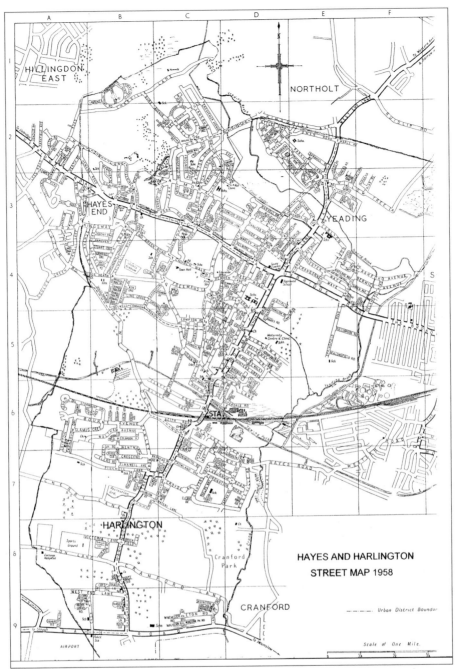

Map of Hayes and Harlington, 1958. The map covers the area that came under the control of the Hayes and Harlington Urban District Council after the reorganisation of local government in 1930. Before then the two parishes had no particular links; they had been in different Poor Law Unions; Hayes had been a separate Urban District since 1904; Harlington, a much smaller parish, was still a rural village which had been part of Staines Rural District. The historical parish boundaries between Hayes and Harlington followed the line of Dawley Road to its junction with North Hyde Road at Bourne's Bridge and then the line of North Hyde Road as far as the River Crane. The boundaries of the new urban district council were for the most part contiguous with the ancient ecclesiastical parishes of Hayes and Harlington. The major exception was the whole eastern boundary of Harlington which was extended to the River Crane so as to include part of what had, until 1930, been the parish of Cranford.

CHAPTER ONE

HAYES

Hayes Town Hall, Wood End, 1950s. The eighteenth-century building, known in 1865 as Grove Lodge, was altered and refaced by Robert Reid in 1871 and renamed Barra Hall. It was purchased by Hayes Urban District Council in 1923 and used as the town hall. The photograph shows the building after a conservatory had been removed from the south side.

Home Farm or Dalton's Farm, Hayes End Road. Although most of the farm buildings shown are mid- to late nineteenth century, the large stable behind the tractor in the photograph is dated at 1810 or earlier.

No. 26 Hayes End Road. This cottage, built around the middle of the nineteenth century, was once a beerhouse. It was later used as a laundry.

Shrubbery Cottages, Hayes End Road. These eighteenth-century cottages stood behind The White Hart public house. They once housed servants at Hayes End House (also known as The Shrubbery) a corner of which can be seen on the left-hand side of the road. The three-bay building adjoining the road appears possibly to be early eighteenth century while the extension, with a curved bay, at the right was perhaps added about the middle of the eighteenth century.

Rose Cottages, Park Lane, 1957. This row of three cottages stood at right angles to the road. Each had simple accommodation of two rooms downstairs and one room upstairs, except for the middle one which had two bedrooms. All three shared a WC. They were demolished a year or so after this photograph was taken.

Uxbridge Road, Hayes End, 1905. The top photograph is of the view looking west. The nearest row of cottages on the right included the shop of Miss Matthews, newsagent and postmistress. The open-top tram in the centre is heading towards Southall and Shepherd's Bush and The Angel Inn can be seen on the left. Note the roadside water pump for watering animals and, in summer, damping down the dust on the road. The photograph below is of the view looking in the opposite direction. Most of the features mentioned above can be seen, although also shown is The Angel's rival – The White Hart – among the buildings in the middle distance. Some horse-drawn traffic, which greatly exceeded mechanically driven vehicles at that time, can be seen in this photograph.

Westcombe Lodge, Uxbridge Road. This house, of no great architectural distinction was demolished in the 1980s, after standing derelict for many years, and replaced by flats. In the First World War it was used by Lady Hillingdon as a hospital for officers. In May 1916 it was reported as having 539 patients.

PLC Engineering Company, Eden Works, Uxbridge Road, 1972. The large building in the photograph was reported to have originally been the stables (with accommodation above for ostlers, grooms, etc.) of the old Adam and Eve coaching inn, behind which it stood. It may well have dated to the early eighteenth century, like the attached house known as Rose Cottage. By about 1910 it had been converted into a factory building, known as the Eden Works, for the Beck Engineering Company which specialised in industrial lamps. By 1922 it was the premises of Marston Billington Ltd, a firm of electrical engineers, and from 1930 onwards it was the premises of the Patent Lighting Company (later PLC Engineering) which manufactured marine lanterns. Following a fire in the late 1970s the factory building was entirely rebuilt but the cottage, a listed building, was restored.

Grange Park Estate, *c.* 1931. This housing estate of 1,280 dwellings, in or near Lansbury Drive, was the first major enterprise of Frank Taylor, later head of Taylor Woodrow the well-known firm of civil engineering contractors. The site was originally Grange (or Whittington's) Farm and the farm buildings can be seen behind the advertisement hoarding. These buildings were used as joiner's shop, stores and site office while the houses were under construction.

Cromwell Avenue *c.* 1935. This photograph shows part of the large housing estate of over 1,000 small private houses built in the late 1920s and '30s by the Allied Building Corporation. The street name (together with Cromwell Road) was inspired by the old Cromwell Cottage which stood nearby in Wood End Green Road. Cromwell Avenue was renamed Commonwealth Avenue in January 1938 at the same time as the other streets in the area were renamed with the titles of royal dynasties that preceded or followed Oliver Cromwell.

Salter Bros. (Smiths and Farriers) Forge, Uxbridge Road, 1956. This must have been a flourishing business in the nineteenth century, with horses to be shod from the Adam and Eve nearby. But by 1956 there was only the occasional horse to deal with. However, the demand for welding and other metal work continued and items such as garden gates were made to order.

Yeading Fever Hospital, 1905. At this time Yeading was still an isolated hamlet in the north-east corner of Hayes parish and the isolation hospital for infectious diseases was in a remote area well away from housing. Known as the Smallpox Hospital in 1919 under the control of the Uxbridge Joint Hospital Board, it was renamed the Isolation Hospital by 1928. It closed down soon afterwards.

Second World War pillbox, Yeading. Now partly hidden by trees, this is the sole remaining pillbox of the ring manned by the Home Guard around the ammunition factory managed by ICI. Thousands of pillboxes were erected all over the country from mid-1940 onwards in anticipation of a German invasion accompanied by a landing by paratroops. This particular example is unusual in that it is a 'double-decker'.

Coldharbour Lane, *c.* 1925. This view, looking south, shows part of the council housing estate on the right and, in the middle distance on the left, some of the buildings of Coldharbour Farm.

Coldharbour Farm, the main yard looking west, 1955. On the right, was the early eighteenth-century farmhouse, a grain store and a barn. Beyond was a porched barn which bore the date '1805' on a tie-beam.

Gravel pits, Hayes, *c.* 1907. Much of Hayes lies over gravel beds created by the prehistoric course of the River Thames. The gravel beds are covered by a variable thickness of brick-earth worked commercially at Botwell and Dawley in the nineteenth and early twentieth centuries but where the gravel is near the surface it was excavated to repair the local roads. The pits shown here were possibly those near the northern edge of Botwell Common – an area threatened recently by an application (refused) for the large-scale commercial excavation of gravel.

Hayes Sewage Disposal Works, 1986. The works were erected in 1902–3 and expanded from time to time. The system of treatment was continuous flow sedimentation followed by percolating filters and humus tanks. The site was reached from Coldharbour Lane by means of a track that is now Minet Drive. The West Middlesex Main Drainage scheme of the 1930s, which created a large modern works at Mogden and an associated sludge disposal works at Perry Oaks, made small sewage works such as this redundant. The buildings had long been derelict when this photograph was taken.

Wood End Green Road, *c.* 1910. These cottages were mainly of mid-eighteenth-century date, although the one at the left had a Regency balcony. The shop was a baker's. The house at the right on the other side of Angel Lane was known as Rosedale.

Angel Lane, 1968. This road linked the High Road by The Angel Inn to Wood End Green Road. The west side of Angel Lane, shown here, was developed well before the east side, the row of cottages dating from about 1840 and the shops probably somewhat earlier.

Morgan's Lane chapel, Hayes End, 1971. Constructed of corrugated iron with neo-Tudor touches, this building opened in 1869 and was used for Christian worship for over 100 years. It was a Baptist church until 1894 when it was purchased by the Wesleyan Methodist congregation who in turn sold the building to Unity Halls and it became a Pentecostal church. The house at the rear of the chapel was added in 1872 and was built originally as a Sunday school. The chapel was demolished in the early 1970s shortly after the photograph was taken.

Rosedale Avenue jubilee celebrations, 1935. The first council houses in Hayes were in a small estate of fifty-one homes which were built in 1913 in Rosedale Avenue, off Wood End Green Road. There was evidently a strong community spirit in this estate, as demonstrated by this procession of children and adults in fancy dress to celebrate the silver jubilee of King George V.

Stephen Storace (1762–96). In the late eighteenth century Storace, although little-known today, enjoyed great popularity as the leading English composer of operas which were played at Drury Lane and all over Britain. He was also a talented musician and a friend of Haydn and Mozart. His sister Nancy played the part of Susanna in the first production of the *Marriage of Figaro* in Vienna in 1786. He married in 1788 and came to live in Hayes at Grove Cottage, later known as The Chestnuts (see below).

The Chestnuts, Wood End. This house was the home of Stephen Storace for about eight years before his death. It was probably built in the early to mid-eighteenth century and was later extended on the west side (on the right in the photograph). In accordance with late eighteenth-century fashion, most of the windows in the entrance front were 'gothicised' and the ogee arches shown were cut into the original brickwork. The house ultimately became the property of Hayes and Harlington Urban District Council which demolished it in 1963.

Town Hall Park, 1930s. Barra Hall and its grounds were acquired by Hayes Urban District Council in 1923 and subsequently converted into offices as the town hall (*see* p. 7). The grounds were laid out as a public park, including a children's playground and paddling pool. A bandstand, seen in the distance, was erected in 1928.

Hayes Silver Band, *c.* 1929. This amateur brass band was formed in 1929 and the photograph must have been taken in the very early days of its existence, before the bandsmen acquired uniforms. They are posed in front of the newly erected bandstand in the Town Hall Park. The band became successful, gaining promotion by 1951 from fifth to championship section of the London and Home Counties Amateur Bands Association and maintaining that position for five consecutive years.

Wood End Green Road, *c.* 1905. This view looking west shows Botwell Lane leading off to the left. The Queen's Head, a small beerhouse, is near the corner and beyond a row of cottages set back out of sight was the White House.

Nos 1, 2 and 3 Clarke's Rents, Wood End. These cottages occupied a walled enclave adjoining Barra Hall Park. They appear to date from the early nineteenth century but little is known of their history.

Beehive Cottages, Church Walk. This row of cottages must have been built some time between 1866 and 1895, as they are shown in the Ordnance Survey map of the later date. Simple dwellings, let at 8s 10d (44p) per week in 1922, they had two advantages – long front gardens and, for sports enthusiasts, they backed on to the Hayes cricket ground.

Dr Triplett's School, Church Walk, c. 1960. The Church of England school was built in 1863, partly subsidised by a charity founded by Dr Thomas Triplett of Hayes. An infants' school was added later. The school was demolished in 1969 after a modern replacement had been built close by in Hemmen Lane.

The parish church of St Mary, Hayes, 1792 and 1795. These copies of watercolour paintings are among the earliest known views of Hayes. The top view, from the south-east and dated 1792, is one of several produced, probably by the same artist, between about 1792 and 1800. It is reasonably accurate, although artistic licence has created the prominent mound on which the church is shown to be standing. The drawing is much as the church appears today except that the pitch of the roof over the south aisle was altered in a Victorian restoration. The lower view by a different artist and believed to date from about 1795, is from the east and is less accurate in detail, for example, the chancel window tracery is wrong and the height of the south aisle gable has been exaggerated. If there was then indeed a field near the east end of the church, as shown, it has since been taken over as an extension of the churchyard. (Pictures courtesy of the Guildhall Library)

Hawthorns High School for Boys – staff and pupils, *c.* 1932. This group photograph shows the head teacher, Mr Eric Blair (right), better known by his later pen-name of George Orwell, with Mr Grey his assistant on the left. The school building was one half of a pair of houses now united as the Fountain House Hotel in Church Road. This bears a plaque stating that George Orwell the famous author taught at the school there between 1932 and 1933.

Little Dawley, Church Road, 1930s. The parents of four pupils at the Hawthorns High School allowed Eric Blair to take the boys of the school for cricket practice in the grounds of this eighteenth-century house which was demolished in 1973.

Hayes Congregational church, 1957. The first building on this site opened as Hayes Town Chapel in 1790 about two years after the founding of the congregation. Due to internal dissension the building was unoccupied or used for storage from 1829 to 1842. When it reopened, the name was changed to Hayes Congregational church and the building was extended during the 1840s. A serious fire in 1947 led to the church being closed for a year. It was rebuilt, but then a new church was constructed nearby – this was completed in 1955 and the old church was demolished in 1959. The Chapel House shown at the left of the photograph was joined on to the chapel's south wall and there is reason to believe that this house was, or formed part of, the original 1790 chapel. This eighteenth-century house, in a conservation area, was demolished in 1997 despite public protest.

Freeman's Lane, nos 10 and 12 in the course of demolition, 1959. These little houses probably dated from the eighteenth century and were a mixture of brick and weatherboard construction. The house beyond (also later demolished) dated from about 1840 and was, it is believed, used as a cottage hospital.

Botwell Mission Football Club. The first eleven for the 1913/14 season posing outside the Botwell Mission Hall – now part of Hayes Library – in Golden Crescent. The team had a very successful season in 1913/14, winning the Uxbridge and District League Cup, the Middlesex & Bucks Advertiser Cup and the Southall Charity Cup. Hayes has had a good record in producing top class footballers and a number of players in the Premiership and First Divisions in the last few years have been born or had their first footballing experience in Hayes. The names of the group are back row, left to right: C. Wright, W. Ramsey, G. Willmott, G. Bird; middle row: A. Harris (Honorary Secretary), J. Fuell, J. Fuell, A. Sceeny, A. Clark, F. George, W. Pudney, J. Burdett, C. Connolly (Trainer); front row: E.W. Shackle (President), F. Knight, C. Ramsey, F. Long (Vice Captain), W. Vaughan, J. West (Captain), Revd Finch (Treasurer).

Hambro Arms, Dawley Road, 1920s. The photograph shows a large group about to set off on a charabanc outing outside the Hambro Arms. A map of 1866 shows a house called Hambro Cottage next to the pub and part of its public bar as Wainwright's grocer's shop. The cottage was later demolished and the pub's entrance now stands in its place.

Botwell House, Botwell Lane *c.* 1910. The early nineteenth-century house was the seat of Edward Nield Shackle who was one of the principal landowners in Hayes. He sold it in 1912 for £4,000 to the Claretian Missionaries, a Roman Catholic community recently established in Hayes. The drawing room – the white single-storey extension at the side of the house – was soon converted into a chapel. The growth in the local Catholic population by 1920 necessitated an extension to the rear of the chapel and then a large addition at the side was made to accommodate up to 600 people. This 'intermediate church' as it was called was superseded by an entirely new church with a tall campanile nearby, which was consecrated in 1972. The bottom photograph shows the interior of the original 'drawing room chapel'.

Botwell Brotherhood Hall, Nield Road, *c.* 1915. The Botwell Brotherhood, an interdenominational Christian association, was founded in 1913. Meeting at first in the then disused cinema, in 1915 the Brotherhood decided to build its own meeting hall. The building work was carried out by the members themselves in their spare time. By 1928 membership had increased to about 200 and the hall had to be enlarged. It still proved to be too small and so the present Central Hall in Coldharbour Lane was opened in 1932. The old site in Nield Road (later renamed St Anselm's Road) was acquired for the Hayes General Post Office. The photograph shows members of the Brotherhood working on their original hall, then in an advanced state of construction.

Carnival procession, Blyth Road, 1918. The Gramophone Company's workers held a sports day carnival on 20 July 1918 at Botwell. There were demonstrations by the Boy Scouts and a Japanese stilt walker, among others. The fancy-dress parade finished with a procession along Blyth Road past the Gramophone factory buildings, as shown in the photograph. The significance of the date is not at all obvious. There was a severe flu epidemic at that time, but the late German offensive on the Western Front had been defeated and perhaps there was a feeling that the end of the war was in sight.

Recording studios of The Gramophone Company, *c.* 1915. Sir Harry Lauder (1870–1950), the famous Scottish comedian and singer made his first recording for The Gramophone Company in 1902. This photograph was taken before the introduction of electrical recording in 1925. It shows the primitive acoustic method which had been in use with little modification since the company started to make records in 1898. It required a performer to sing into a horn only a few inches away from his face and produced records that by the 1920s, with the introduction of radio broadcasting, were sounding increasingly antiquated. (Photograph courtesy of EMI plc)

'His Master's Voice'. Artist Francis Barraud made several copies of his best-known work 'His Master's Voice'. The dog in the painting was a stray fox terrier, Nipper, who had belonged to Barraud's brother. In 1899 Barraud visited the London offices of The Gramophone Company (which moved to Hayes in 1907 and is now EMI) with a painting of Nipper listening to a wax-cylinder recording of 'His Master's Voice'. He showed it to the managing director who agreed to buy it if Barraud would replace the cylinder phonograph with a painting of one of the company's gramophones. The painting was made the trade mark of The Gramophone Company and attained such fame that the organisation became better known by the initials 'HMV'. EMI abandoned the use of the HMV trade mark on its records from 1990 but the name survives in the company's chain of HMV shops. (Photograph courtesy of EMI plc)

Blyth Road, Botwell, *c.* 1910. This view from Hayes Station Bridge shows some of the privately built housing constructed in around 1906 and intended primarily to accommodate workers from the factories of the Hayes Development Company's industrial estate in Clayton Road and Blyth Road. The nearest row of nine houses is Priory Villas and the next six (after the semi-detached pair), are known as South View. In the distance can be seen the buildings of The Gramophone Company and, on the left, the factory of the Goss Printing Press Company, a firm from Chicago, USA, which purchased the site in 1904 and started operating by about 1906.

The McCurd Lorry Manufacturing Co. Ltd, 1927. The Goss Printing Press Company's works was occupied during the First World War by the National Aero Engine Factory. It was taken over in 1921 by the McCurd Lorry Manufacturing Co. which moved from Edgware Road. As well as lorries with a 4-ton capacity the firm also produced three models of charabancs and a 12/20 hp motor car. The company was wound-up in 1927 and was said to have priced itself out of the market. The motto in the advertisement shown here could well be taken to heart by at least two of the giant manufacturers of motor cars today.

British Electric Transformer Company, Clayton Road, 1960s. This was the first large factory to be opened in Hayes, starting up in Clayton Road in 1901 having moved from Paddington. Although transformers were the most important product, electrical equipment of all kinds from kettles upwards was also manufactured by BET. A 200-ton crane was introduced to handle the heaviest transformers and these, when towed on low-loaders through the streets of Hayes, tended to cause traffic jams. The factory also had a rail link with the Great Western Railway main line, which crossed Station Road immediately south of the canal. BET was eventually absorbed by Crompton Parkinson and then in turn by the Hawker Siddeley Group. The photograph shows a transformer on a low-loader leaving the Clayton Road factory.

The X-Chair Patent Co. Ltd, Silverdale Road, c. 1913. The firm was founded in 1897, then a site in Hayes was purchased in 1907 and a new factory began production on this site in 1909. An important product of the firm was a folding camp chair which when opened formed an 'X', but all kinds of folding equipment was produced, including cake-stands! The firm celebrated its golden jubilee in 1947 with a river trip to Windsor for all its staff but within ten years the factory had closed.

Coal deliveries, Botwell, *c.* 1912. The Lilleshall Company Ltd is listed in *Kelly's Directory* (Middlesex) for 1910 and 1914 but not 1917 or later. This coal merchant's business was based at Hayes station, so judging from the load, the coalman and his patient horse pictured outside the Railway Arms must be somewhere near the beginning of their round.

Station Hill, Hayes, 1920s. Men from the nearby factories sit eating their sandwiches during the lunch-time break. The hut shown just right of centre is believed to have been a Wesleyan chapel and the large board, left of centre, is inscribed 'T.S. Rose, Atlas Cycle Works'. The bicycle became an increasingly popular means of transport for factory workers in the 1920s to 1950s. The double-headed cart drawn by two horses heading up the hill is presumably carrying an extra heavy load.

Aerial view of EMI factory complex, looking north from a vantage point to the south of the railway line, 1970. Most of the factory buildings in the photograph are part of the EMI complex which, at its zenith, occupied an area of 150 acres. EMI started life as The Gramophone Company which moved to a site next to the railway line at Botwell in 1907. It soon began to expand and after a merger with the Columbia Graphophone Company in 1931 the holding company became known as EMI, although The Gramophone Company continued in name as a subsidiary of EMI until 1973. The photograph shows the extent to which the factory complex had grown by 1970 when 16,000 people were employed there. Dawley Road, which historically is the boundary between Hayes on the right and the Dawley area of Harlington on the

left, splits the view approximately in half. On the left of the road the buildings include the Rudge Whitworth factory, immediately north of the railway line; this was built in the late 1930s when the company moved from Coventry following its acquisition by EMI. Rudge Whitworth was sold to Raleigh Industries in the mid-1940s and the factory building was occupied by EMI Electronics. Further expansion of the Dawley site occurred later but by the time this photograph was taken redevelopment had already begun. Since then the whole area has been redeveloped and few of the buildings on the left of the photograph remain. A similar fate awaits the large factory buildings on the right, which are redundant and scheduled for demolition.

GB 84 42 b
mit GB 80 17 b

Nur für den Dienstgebrauch

Bild Nr. 663/40 (Lfl. 3) 138

Aufnahme vom 15. 8. 40

Hayes

Funkgeräte „Marconi Ltd."
mit GB 80 17 Motorradfabrik „Rudge-Withworth"

Länge (westl. Greenw.): 0° 25′ 56″ Breite: 51° 30′ 00″ (Bildmitte)
Mißweisung: — 10° 07′ (Mitte 1942) Zielhöhe über NN 30 m

Maßstab etwa 1 : 17 300

Genst. 5. Abt.   März 19

Karte 1 : 100 000

GB/E 34

Hayes and Harlington from the air, 1940. During the early years of the Second World War, the Luftwaffe undertook the photography of the whole of Britain and its survey is the best aerial record of the country up to 1940. The original of this photograph was taken on 5 August 1940 and this edited version was prepared in March 1942 to identify the location of the EMI and Rudge Whitworth factories. Curiously EMI is misidentified as radio manufacturer 'Marconi Ltd'; possibly because the company, as well as making radios and televisions under its HMV trade mark, also used the lesser-known 'Marconiphone' trade mark for its cheaper models. Rudge Whitworth is misidentified as a manufacturer of motorcycles; in fact, the company had ceased to make them soon after the outbreak of war, although the Germans could be forgiven for not knowing this. A similar photograph to identify the exact position of the Fairey Aviation Company's factory in North Hyde Road was also prepared. Both photographs were obtained from captured German archives at the end of the war. Although the caption describes it as Hayes, the area covered by the photograph actually shows most of Harlington and Sipson and only the southern half of Hayes.

CHAPTER TWO

HARLINGTON

Dawley Manor Farm, c. 1905. This is a view of the farmhouse taken from the junction of Cherry Lane (now St Paul's Close) and Harlington High Street (now St Peter's Way); the man standing in the doorway is the owner, R.P. Newman. The attractive farmhouse with its fine barns dated from the sixteenth century but was demolished in 1961 to make way for the M4 motorway – the only building in Harlington to suffer this fate. The name of the farm is puzzling because this part of Harlington never formed part of the manor of Dawley. Some historians have even confused it with Dawley House, the palatial eighteenth-century manor house of Dawley. This stood about half a mile further north and its one-time owner, Lord Bolingbroke, was pleased to refer to his house as 'Dawley Farm'.

Fairey Aviation Company's factory, North Hyde Road, *c*. 1920. The Fairey Aviation Company was building aircraft at premises in Clayton Road, Hayes in 1915 but even after its main works were established in North Hyde Road, just in Harlington, it retained Hayes as its postal address. This early aerial photograph shows Station Road on the left before the houses which now line the eastern side road were built. At this time Station Road joined, but did not immediately cross, North Hyde Road. To reach the station it was necessary to turn sharp right and then left where Station Road continued along what is now Old Station Road. What appears to be the continuation of Station Road beyond the crossroads in the photograph is in fact Albert Road with Elim church on the left. This road then continues into Keith Road where only six pairs of semi-detached houses had, as yet, been built.

North Hyde Road area, *c*. 1950. This oblique aerial photograph is a view from above Hayes station looking in south-westerly direction. The Fairey Aviation factory occupies the middle part of the photograph. Beyond are houses in Dawley Road and the Pinkwell estate and in the far distance is Heathrow Airport still under construction. The factory opened in North Hyde Road during the First World War and gradually expanded, reaching its fullest extent at about the time this photograph was taken. The works were closed in 1972 and the site is now an industrial estate.

Demolition of Fairey factory, 1973. The Luftwaffe failed to do any substantial damage to the Fairey Aviation factory. The most serious damage to the company was in fact accomplished by the Air Ministry which seized the company's airfield at Heathrow in 1944 (*see* pp. 125–6) under the pretext that it was required for military purposes. The loss of the airfield and the protracted legal arguments over compensation that followed affected the company's viability to such a degree that it was taken over by Westland Aircraft Ltd in 1960. Westland closed the factory in 1972 and moved production to its headquarters at Yeovil, Somerset. Most of the site, except for the office buildings in North Hyde Road, was then cleared in 1973 to make way for an industrial estate.

Bedwell House, Station Road, 1968. This house, built in the latter part of the nineteenth century for Charles Newman, now stands rather forlornly, surrounded by modern developments. It stood well back from the road, then known as Bedwell Lane, and was surrounded by a large garden. It lost its garden in the 1930s when the houses in Bedwell Gardens (then a cul-de-sac) were built and some of these can be seen on the left. In 1964, as part of the diversions caused by the construction of the M4, Bedwell Gardens became part of the main thoroughfare between Hayes and Harlington.

Harlington Splash, c. 1930. Much better known as Jessop's Pond, it was at the northern end of the High Street just past its junction with Cherry Lane and immediately to the north of Dawley Manor Farm. It took its name from Joseph Jessop who owned the farm in the early nineteenth century. Soon after the photograph was taken a motorcyclist ran off the road into the pond on a foggy night and was drowned; as a result the pool was filled in. The M4 motorway now crosses the foreground of the photograph and the fire station occupies the area on the right just beyond the pond.

War Memorial, Cherry Lane Cemetery. The worst incident of the war in Hayes occurred in the afternoon of 7 July 1944 when a V-1 flying bomb hit one of the surface air-raid shelters of The Gramophone Company (EMI). In the words of an air-raid warden, who recorded the incident in his diary, 'the wings started to wobble from side to side as it lost flying speed and then came in a dive at the entrance to the shelter. Some of the seriously injured and dead were got out of the emergency exit but many were trapped for hours under the ten inch thick concrete roof which had collapsed on top of them. The next shelter had its top lifted and moved over but not quite enough for it to fall in.' The monument records the names of the 37 people killed in the incident, 12 of whom were buried together in the cemetery.

Church Hall, Cherry Lane, c. 1909. The old church hall was built on the north-east corner of the Rectory garden in the early 1900s. With the old Rectory, it was demolished in 1970 when the garden was turned into a housing estate. The houses in St Paul's Close (as this fragment of Cherry Lane is now called) now occupy the site. Although generally speaking the redevelopment of the Rectory garden was an environmental disaster, it must be admitted that the new church hall is a distinct improvement on its predecessor.

Church of St Peter and St Paul, Harlington. Above is the south-east view of the twelfth-century church taken from the field opposite. The picture could have been taken at any time between the restoration of the building in 1880 and the construction of the M4 motorway in the early 1960s. The view is no more as, in 1962, the High Street was diverted across the foreground of the photograph. Soon after planning permission was given on appeal for a petrol station to be built between the road and the church and the view of the church from the High Street was obscured forever. The petrol station closed in 1989 and since then the site has had various occupants (below).

Harlington Rectory, 1968. The old Rectory, which was demolished in 1971, had stood on the same site for at least 400 years but had been rebuilt in the late nineteenth century when part of the earlier timber-framed building was incorporated in the central block. When the house was demolished most of the trees on the site were felled and the large garden developed for housing – a development which did irreparable harm to the setting of the church on its northern side. Of the many trees 'protected' by preservation orders, only the large cedar tree survived as even the developers shrank from felling this fine specimen. The top photograph shows the north side of the building, taken from Cherry Lane (St Paul's Close) and gives a good impression of its size and rambling character. The lower photograph, taken from the churchyard, shows the other side of the building, with the fifteenth-century church tower on the right.

The Harlington Yew, *c.* 1770. This painting of the yew tree on the southern side of the church bears a close resemblance to a print of the tree published in 1770. However, unlike the print, the painting includes the church in the background with the turret depicted on the wrong side of the tower (*see* p. 43). This suggests that it was probably painted from memory, with a copy of the print of the tree to hand. The church is also out of proportion to the tree which, at that time, was just over forty feet in height and much shorter than the church tower. According to a rhyme, written in 1729 and which accompanies the 1770 print, the tree was very much as depicted and there is no good reason to doubt the accuracy of the painting in this respect. The rhyme goes on to claim that the tree 'yielded to Arlington a fame much greater than its Earldom's name'. Henry Bennet, the Earl of (H)Arlington, took his title from the village where his father was lord of the manor; no doubt then, as now, the H of Harlington was not always aspirated. The tree is obviously of great age and an examination by the Conservation Foundation in 1990 concluded that it could well be more than 1,000 years old. It was severely damaged in a gale in 1959 and, although still very much alive, it is only a shadow of its former self.

Townsend, Dawley Road, 1971. This was an appropriate name for the house when it was built in 1910. It stood alone at the northern extremity of the village where the High Street becomes Dawley Road. It was still a private house when this photograph was taken but soon after it became a school for children with special needs. It now belongs to the Comfort (formerly Arlington) Hotel, which stands behind the house, and is used as an annexe to the hotel. It is destined to be demolished to make way for an extension to the hotel.

Boys at Dawley Manor Farm, early 1890s. The five boys are standing in a field between Dawley Manor Farm and Church Farm with the rickyard of Dawley Manor Farm in the background. The line of large trees in the background mark the route of Watery Lane which has now been replaced by the M4. The scene is obviously taken in winter; the boys are well-dressed for the occasion and are possibly showing off their Christmas presents. Left to right: Robert Newman (1878–1954), John Newman (1883–1961), Hubert (Bert) Philp of Sipson, William Newman (1882–1917) and Alfred Newman (1887–1917).

Northern end of High Street. The top photograph, taken in 1935, shows the High Street with its junction with Cherry Lane (now St Paul's Close) on the left. On the right is Dawley Manor Farm (*see* p. 37) and to its right, partially obscured by the trees, is a large sixteenth-century barn, part of which can be seen on the left of the photograph on p. 45. The old High Street originally continued further north to join Dawley Road and Station Road at The Great Western but became a cul-de-sac (St Peter's Way) when the M4 motorway was constructed across the old road in 1961. The lower photograph, taken about 1920, shows the view from a point about 200 yards south of the church which is the only building in the picture still remaining. The house on the left is Pear Tree Cottage, next to this one of the large black barns of Philp's farm can just be seen.

J. Saunders and Son, Shoe Repairs. James Saunders started a shoe repair business in Harlington in 1902. His first shop was the end house of a terraced block which stood opposite The Red Lion on the north-east corner of the junction of Sipson Lane and the High Street. When this terrace was converted into one large house, and renamed Gothic House (demolished in the early 1960s and replaced by Gothic Court), the premises were moved to the other side of the High Street. The top photograph shows the shop where James Saunders, followed by his son Cecil, continued the shoe repair business until 1995 when Cecil retired. Between them, father and son served Harlington for more than ninety years. The bottom photograph shows Cecil Saunders and his sister Eileen in the shop in 1986, the interior of the shop and its fittings had changed little in the previous seventy years.

Wicks & Son, *c.* 1983. There was a butcher's shop on this site for more than 100 years but the shop in the picture is clearly of 1930s origin. For most of the first forty years of this century the village butcher was H.S. Ferris but in 1944 ownership passed to W. Wicks & Son. Their shop continued in business until 1983 and the photograph shows Mrs Wicks standing outside the shop shortly before the business changed hands. The premises continued as a butcher's until 1995 but it is unlikely that Harlington will ever again have its own butcher.

Maison Sylvia, *c.* 1942. The hairdresser's shop of this name was acquired by F.W. Hodges in 1938 and the building has continued in his family's ownership ever since. This group was all employed in the shop and includes, at the extreme right, F.W. Hodges himself, his son Ken and his wife, with their three assistants. The 21*s* (£1.05) above the window refers to the price of a lady's perm at that time. It is now The Hair Shop.

Shackle's House, High Street, 1958. This house, which appeared to have had no name other than that of its owner, stood on the east side of the street opposite The White Hart. The main part dated from the early nineteenth century with a wing added later on the north side of the building. The photograph shows the rear of the house with the later wing on the right. The house was demolished in 1960 and the site is now occupied by the flats in Pembury Court.

Harlington High Street, c. 1920. Charles Shackle (1875–1960) and his wife in their 1905 model twin-cylinder 10 hp Rolls-Royce are parked outside Shackle's House. The photograph is obviously posed, a fact made all the more clear by the discovery that at the time it was taken Charles Shackle was unable to drive. His chauffeur, standing next to the car, must have driven it away soon after. Mr Shackle was a civil engineer employed by the Great Western Railway and was the founder and president of the Harlington Locomotive Society.

The Harlington Locomotive Society. In 1947 Charles Shackle, who had by then retired from the Great Western Railway, invited local model railway enthusiasts to join him in the construction of a model railway line on orchard land to the south of his house. This led to the formation of the Harlington Locomotive Society. By 1949 the Society had 432 ft of track which was extended to a length of 1,026 ft in 1954. The top photograph was taken in the early 1950s before the houses in Richard's Close were built in 1958. It shows the track running through what was then a large orchard; it still follows the same route but is now hemmed in by the later developments. The bottom photograph was taken on one of the Society's open days in 1952. The children are being given rides behind a model engine driven by Peter Tarrant; in the background is Woodlands.

Woodlands, High Street, 1958. The former farmhouse, which was demolished in 1960 for no particularly good reason, stood on the west side of the High Street to the south of The White Hart. It was brick-built with a tiled roof, gabled at one end and half-hipped where it faced the road. Although the house had eighteenth-century features it could well have been much older. The site is now occupied by nos 178 to 182 High Street; the barn to the left of the house survives and now serves as a garage for some of the new houses.

Election meeting, High Street, 1906. The group is standing in the middle of the High Street at a meeting prior to the General Election on 18 January 1906; in the background on the right is Woodlands and the barn seen in the previous photograph. The building on the extreme left is the last in the terrace known as Dispensary Cottages. In 1906 both Hayes and Harlington were part of the large constituency of Uxbridge which included most of West Middlesex. It had been represented, in the Conservative cause since 1885 by Sir Frederick Dixon-Hartland who is the elderly man, with a beard and wearing a trilby hat, in the centre of the photograph. His wife is sitting in the car and on his left is his local agent R.P. Newman. Uxbridge was regarded as a safe Conservative seat but Dixon-Hartland survived the Liberal landslide of 1906 with a majority of only 145.

Harlington Pond. The top photograph is very faded but is included here because of its great historical interest. Taken in 1866, it is the earliest known photograph of Harlington and as such it is also the only record that we have of the lock-up which is the small circular building on the extreme right. The lock-up for the temporary imprisonment of criminals had been built in 1798 at the instigation of the Rector, the Revd B. Gabriel and had the slogan 'Live and Repent' over the door. A very similar lock-up still survives in Cranford High Street. To the left of this is the village pound when it was still being used to secure stray animals. The building behind the lock-up is Manor Farm which was completely rebuilt soon after (*see* p. 56). The lower photograph shows much the same area in the 1920s. The old Baptist church can be seen through the trees and to the right of this is Chapel Row which appears in both photographs.

Harlington Baptist church. The old Baptist church (above) has four distinct parts which show how it has been extended since it was first built in the 1770s. At that time it belonged to a nonconformist group which formally became a Baptist church in 1798. The oldest part is at the extreme left and, until it was removed and placed inside the church, the wooden lintel above the doorway to this part bore the crudely carved inscription 'JA 1775 SH'. The middle part was added very soon after; on the external wall one of the bricks has the inscription 'HT 1779'. Further additions were made until the Baptists ran out of space and opened a new church on the opposite side of the road in 1879. This building is shown in the lower photograph which was taken during the centenary celebrations of the church in 1898. The old building still belongs to the Baptist church and it was restored as the Frank Peace Hall (the name of a former minister) in 1975. The outside of the building has changed little in the last 100 years.

Members of Harlington Baptist church, 1898. Members of the church posed for this picture during the church's centenary celebrations. In the centre is John Heyward, a well-known local farmer, and seated in front of him and holding an umbrella is his wife, Elizabeth. The ladies to the left and right of Mrs Heyward are, respectively, Miss S. Philp and Mrs Eldridge. The lady wearing a shawl in front of Miss Philp is believed to be Mrs French. The lady at the extreme right is believed to be Miss Hawthorn and the man in the back row, second from the left is Mr Eldridge. The group seems to be unaware that they are being observed by a number of children whose faces can just be seen peering through the shrubbery!

Opposite: The Lilacs, High Street, 1960s. This stood just to the south of Cedar Cottages (which can just be seen to its right) and was reputedly the home of William Byrd, the Elizabethan composer, when he lived in Harlington between 1577 and 1593. The photograph was taken after the pond had been filled in in the early 1960s, but before the house was demolished in 1968. In the mid-nineteenth century the house was known as Overburg House and was operated as a boys' boarding school under the name of 'Mr. Webster's Academy for Young Gentlemen'. By 1861 Joseph Smith had become the proprietor of the Academy and had twenty-five boys, aged between six and nineteen in residence. On his retirement in 1873 it became a private house and remained so until its demolition.

Cedar Cottages, High Street, 1970. This group of three cottages, now numbered 268, 270 and 272 High Street, with the adjoining Baptist church form an attractive feature in the centre of the village. The houses date from the late seventeenth century and were probably originally one building which was later divided into three.

Village centre, *c.* 1910. This photograph was taken from a point slightly to the south of the buildings that appear on pp. 52–3. All the buildings can be recognised from the previous illustrations with the exception of Manor Farm standing to the right of Chapel Row. Comparison of this with the earlier photograph shows that it must have been completely rebuilt. It was demolished in the mid-1930s when the shops in Manor Parade were built. Only the Baptist church and manse survive.

Sunnyside Cottages, High Street, 1958. These cottages dated from the early nineteenth century. They were originally called Sapperton Row, but locally they were known as 'the nine houses'. They were demolished in 1958 and replaced by the houses now numbered as 355 to 365 High Street. On the far left of the photograph is Wicks' butcher's shop (*see* p. 48).

The Dower House, High Street, 1958. The front which faces the High Street was built in the early sixteenth century; the wing extending to the rear was added later in the same century and was extended still further in the eighteenth century. The house is timber-framed with a brick fronting which was added later. Apart from the church, it is probably the oldest building in Harlington. The origin of the name is unknown as it was never used as a dower house by any of the local landed families.

Harlington Senior School, New Road, 1929. Middlesex County Council was one of the most progressive education authorities in the country. Fifteen years before the 1944 Education Act was passed, Middlesex already had the kind of education system which the Act was intended to establish. Before then most children started lessons at the age of five and remained in the same school until the age of fourteen. The Middlesex system introduced senior schools to which children transferred at the age of eleven. New schools were built throughout the county and this photograph was taken just before the school in New Road opened in 1929. Children over the age of eleven, who had previously attended the schools in Harmondsworth, Sipson and Harlington, transferred to the new school unless they passed the examination to go to one of the county grammar schools. After 1944 the school was renamed Harlington Secondary Modern School and it became a comprehensive school in the 1970s. It was replaced by Harlington Community School in Pinkwell Lane and demolished in 1995.

A reaping and binding machine, a relic of the agricultural past of the area, lays abandoned in 1971 in a field just to the south of the M4; the field has since become a gravel pit (*see* p. 59). These machines revolutionised harvesting when they were introduced in the latter half of the nineteenth century. Previously the work had been done by hand with sickles and scythes. They were made obsolete by the introduction of combine harvesters one of which is shown below working in the same area with the bulk of the Forte Crest Hotel in the distance. The more modern machine completed the harvesting in less than two days.

Gravel excavation, 1978. Most of the land around Harlington and Harmondsworth is Grade 1 agricultural land which is ideally suited to growing virtually any type of crop. Although only 2.5 per cent of the land in Britain is classified as Grade 1, this has not prevented gravel extraction replacing agriculture as the principal land use in the locality. This shows the ugly scars caused by the gravel workings in the area of the previous photograph. Rising behind them is the even uglier Forte Crest Hotel. Permission to build this monstrosity was allowed on appeal in 1969, on the grounds that an hotel standing about 120 ft would do no violence to the M4 or its surroundings!

Picking strawberries at Heyward's Farm, 1906. Women from Shropshire came regularly each year to pick strawberries and other soft fruit which were grown in West Middlesex for the London market. After picking the fruit early in the morning it had to be sorted and packed into punnets ready for market. After packing, the fruit was rushed off to Hayes station to be put on the train to London. Some was taken direct to Covent Garden by horse-drawn strawberry vans, a special type of lightweight wagon for rapid transport to market.

Watersplash Lane, *c.* 1935. This lane originally led from North Hyde Road to Church Road, Cranford. It forded the River Crane at a point where, for a short distance, the river was the boundary between the ancient parishes of Harlington and Cranford. The left side of the bridge is in Harlington and the right side is in Cranford. The ford from which the lane derives its name is hidden from view by the footbridge. The rural aspect of the lane seen in this picture has since been completely destroyed. The road was first cut in two by the construction of the Parkway and then cut again by the construction of the M4 so it is now a dead end and no longer serves as a short cut to Cranford. Until the road bridge was built in the mid-1930s North Hyde Road, which is only 200 yd to the north, also forded the Crane. Because of their close proximity, old photographs of the two fords are frequently confused.

Cranford Lane, *c.* 1960. The centres of the villages of Heston, Cranford, Harlington, Sipson and Harmondsworth are well to the north of the Bath Road and are linked together by a lane which runs parallel to it. Cranford Lane is the central part of the link and this photograph shows the lane before it was urbanised and gravel excavation began in the fields on either side. Brockley Cottages (1888), Richmond Cottages (1891) and Henley Cottages, the first houses (now nos 100 to 122 Cranford Lane) at the Harlington end of the lane, are in the middle distance.

Cranford Lane, *c.* 1910. This photograph was taken about half a mile to the east of the previous illustration at a point where the road, soon after leaving Cranford High Street, runs parallel to the River Crane for a short distance before crossing the river and proceeding on its way to Harlington. Since 1930 the river has officially been the boundary between Harlington and Cranford, although the ancient boundary between the two is halfway along the lane. The two people in the photograph, on the Cranford side of the river, are Mrs Shackle of Harlington (*see* p. 49) and one of her sons – boys at that time were often dressed in what would now be regarded as effeminate clothes.

Ash Cottage, Bath Road, 1967. This early nineteenth century house stood on the Bath Road to the east of The Coach and Horses and almost opposite The Crown (*see* p. 63). It was demolished in the early 1970s and the Ibis Hotel now occupies the site. The tree on the left of the photograph was spared and it now stands in front of the hotel.

The Coach and Horses, Harlington Corner, 1910. The title of this faded photograph could refer either to the inn or the coach and horses standing outside. The old coaching inn, dating from the late eighteenth century, was the best known and most attractive of the public houses in Harlington. It was needlessly demolished when the Ariel Hotel (since renamed the Post House Hotel) was built behind it in 1961. In 1830 about forty-five stagecoaches and four mail coaches passed the Coach and Horses in each direction every day. With the opening of the railway the service collapsed and was withdrawn in 1843. The coach and horses seen in the photograph must therefore have been special visitors. Standing on either side of the doorway of the inn are the licensee T.E. Ryan and his wife; the little girl standing on the seat is their daughter Ena.

The Pheasant, West End Lane, c. 1910. This public house, which dates from the late eighteenth century, is now the oldest in Harlington. At the time of this photograph the hamlet of West End was separated from Harlington by the length of West End Lane and The Pheasant was the first building encountered on the way from Harlington. The elm trees disappeared in the 1930s to make way for the houses in The Crescent.

The Red Lion, High Street, *c.* 1960. This prominent landmark, at the centre of the village, dates from about 1840. The front facing the High Street is the oldest part, with numerous additions added between 1840 and the end of the century. Soon after this photograph was taken the brickwork was painted over as part of a misguided scheme on the part of the brewers to make all their public houses look as alike as possible. Fortunately the unique etched glass windows were retained. Standing to the right of the building are Ratcliffe's Cottages which were demolished in the early 1970s and replaced by modern houses numbered as 293 to 297 High Street.

The Crown, Bath Road, *c.* 1960. Like The Red Lion this public house also dates from the early Victorian period with later additions. However, unlike its contemporary, it has suffered the indignity of being facetiously renamed The Office. Planning permission was given in 1997 for its conversion into a small hotel which, if implemented, will considerably change its appearance. The Crown stood almost opposite the Coach and Horses (*see* p. 62).

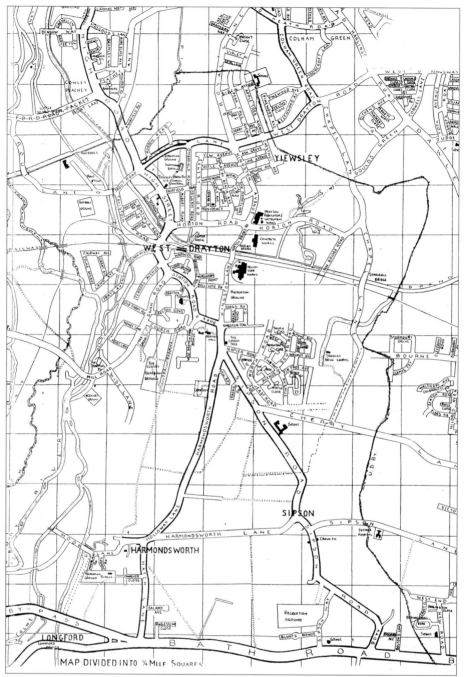

Map of Yiewsley and West Drayton area, 1948. The Urban District of Yiewsley and West Drayton was formed in 1930 by the amalgamation of Yiewsley Urban District Council, West Drayton Parish Council and Harmondsworth Parish Council. This map shows most of the area which came under the new jurisdiction. It included the urbanised areas of Yiewsley and West Drayton in the north and the still rural villages of Harmondsworth, Sipson, Longford and Heathrow in the south. The photographs in the remaining chapters of this book were taken within the area covered by the map. The urban district council was dissolved on 1 April 1965 and became part of the London Borough of Hillingdon.

CHAPTER THREE

YIEWSLEY

Yiewsley Town Hall. The building was opened in May 1930 to provide accommodation for the newly formed Yiewsley and West Drayton Urban District Council. It is shown here during the Second World War with a poster advertising events for 'Workers Holidays at Home'. The town hall ceased to serve its original function when the Council acquired Drayton Hall as its administrative headquarters in the early 1950s. With the formation of the London Borough of Hillingdon in 1965, Drayton Hall was sold for private development but the old town hall continues in use as council offices.

Falling Lane. The top photograph, taken about 1900, shows the Nag's Head – a nineteenth-century public house which stands at the corner of Falling Lane and Royal Lane. The lower photograph, of about 1930, shows the houses seen above on the left with the late 1920s council homes which form part of the large estate in this part of Yiewsley. The origin of the name Falling Lane is obscure but on some nineteenth-century maps it is shown as Felling Lane.

Yiewsley Grange, 1939. This large house is located at the northern boundary of Yiewsley parish where the Cowley Road crosses the River Pinn. The building is listed Grade II and dates from about 1600, its original timber framing being encased in brick. During the nineteenth century it was known as Brookside but early in the twentieth century was renamed Yiewsley Grange. The photograph shows it in August 1939 when it was still a private house; in recent years it has been turned into offices.

Rabb's Corner, *c.* 1900. This was the name of the crossroads at the north end of Yiewsley High Street, the junction of Trout Road, Falling Lane and the continuation of the High Street called Cowley Road. It was named after the adjacent Rabb's Farm but was also known as The Pump. In this view of about 1900, the George and Dragon can be seen on the right and on the left is the village pump which gave the junction its alternative name. If it were not for the continued presence of the pub the view today would be difficult to locate.

Yiewsley Ford, early 1900s. This crossing of the River Colne by Ford Road (an extension of Packet Boat Lane) was known as Yiewsley Ford although when Yiewsley parish was established it was slightly north of the parish boundary.

Yiewsley Methodist churches. The former Wesleyan church (top) in Yiewsley High Street dates from 1872 and is seen here about 1900. It was the home of the Methodist congregation until 1927 when the new Central Hall, seen in the lower photograph, was opened. The older building was converted to house the Yiewsley branch of Middlesex County Libraries from 1931 until 1973 and now provides office accommodation. The Methodist Central Hall, in Fairfield Road, Yiewsley was opened on 31 August 1927 and is seen here in the following year. The hall seated 600 and was often used for concerts and other events. It was demolished in 1972, to make way for a supermarket, and replaced by a smaller hall nearby in 1973.

Yiewsley Recreation Ground. The recreation ground occupies most of the rectangle formed by the High Street, Falling Lane, Otterfield Road and Fairfield Road and is an attractive feature in the middle of the town. The swimming pool, seen in 1960, lies on its southern edge and was opened in July 1934. It was originally open to the elements but was roofed-in in 1976. The bowling green (below) was opened by the Yiewsley and West Drayton urban district council in the 1930s. In 1996 Hillingdon Council seriously considered the sale of the recreation ground for a superstore development but, after intense local opposition, the plan was abandoned in July 1997.

Marathon race, Yiewsley High Street, 1908. The Olympic Games held in London in July 1908 generated a nationwide interest in long-distance running and many local 'Marathon Races' were organised in the following months. This Yiewsley Marathon was a 10-mile race held on Saturday 5 September 1908. It started from near the De Burgh Arms Hotel and the runners are seen here running along Yiewsley High Street towards Cowley. The route continued to Iver, Langley, Thorney and once round West Drayton Green before finishing at a point in Yiewsley High Street close to the start. It was won by W. Hoare of Southall in a time of 70 min 4.4 sec.

St Matthew's Football Team, 1906/7. The vicar of St Matthew's, the Revd F.D. Sturgess is seated in the middle; in front of him is the team captain, Frank Green, who was head of Padcroft Boys' Home (see p. 72). The only other member of the team who has been identified is Bill Orchard on the extreme left at the front.

Padcroft Boys' Home, above *c.* 1920, below 1931. The site for the boys' home had been occupied by a private school from 1874 until about 1900 when the buildings were acquired by the Church of England Temperance Society for use as a home for 'boys of the hooligan class'. The home was later transferred to the London Police Court Mission. Mr Frank Green (*see* p. 71) was manager from its opening in 1902 until its closure in 1949. Most of the original buildings were destroyed by fire in 1905 but they were quickly rebuilt. The lower picture shows the new extension designed by local architect Mr Hubert F. Bateman.

The Yiewsley and West Drayton Silver Prize Band, 1925. Founded in 1890 as the Wesleyan Band of Hope Brass Band, it became the Yiewsley Brass Band in 1894 and then the Yiewsley and West Drayton Prize Band in 1906.

High Street, *c.* 1930. View looking north towards the canal bridge; the entrance to the railway station approach is on the right. Johnson's Wax factory had occupied Colham Wharf (built 1796) since 1919. Rudlings hardware store can be seen on the left. The shops, then occupied by W.H. Smith & Son and the pharmacy of W. Luty Wells, still survive but all the other buildings have been demolished.

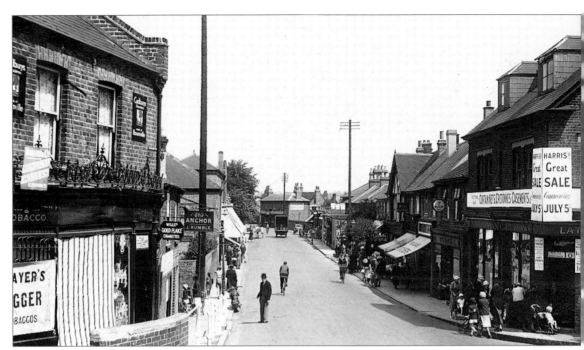

High Street, *c.* 1935. View looking north from the canal bridge; on the left is The Anchor public house, the blacksmith's and the Co-operative Stores (*see* p. 76). On the other side of the road in the distance is The Red Cow public house (*see* p. 75) and in the foreground Harris's the drapers.

Barclay's Bank and De Burgh Arms Hotel, *c.* 1970. These buildings stand on either side of Station Approach at its junction with the High Street. Barclay's Bank has been housed in a variety of buildings on this site since 1905. The De Burgh Arms Hotel dates from the seventeenth century but it has been much altered over the years.

The Red Cow, High Street, 1961. This was a nineteenth-century public house, shown here one year before it was demolished and replaced by a modern building with the same name.

Street Market, High Street, 1930s. The yard adjacent to The Red Cow provided a site for a flourishing greengrocery and fruit market. It is said that in the early years of the twentieth century the yard was the venue for street entertainers and cheapjacks on Saturday evenings.

Yiewsley Co-op, 1976. The Yiewsley and West Drayton Co-operative Society opened a store on this site in Yiewsley in March 1908. It was extended in 1934 and became part of the London Co-operative Society. The parade of shops included a drapery store, shoe shop, grocer's, butcher's and greengrocer's above which was a Co-op hall. It is shown here in 1976 soon after its closure; it was then replaced by a new building incorporating a Co-operative supermarket.

High Street, c. 1930. View looking south with the canal bridge in the distance. The shops on the left were built on to the front of residential properties. All have now been replaced except the one on the extreme left which was then the Yiewsley Post Office; this still survives with its decorative columns.

High Street, *c*. 1950. View looking north from the corner of Fairfield Road. The shops on the right were built about 1937 and on the left is the Marlborough cinema which was opened in September 1923 and enlarged in 1933. It was renamed the Ritz in 1956 and finally closed in April 1960.

High Street, *c*. 1950. View looking north: on the right is The Red Cow with its adjoining street market (*see* p. 75). In the distance is the town hall at the corner of Fairfield Road (*see* p. 65). To the left of the tree is St Matthew's church.

High Street, 1920s. View looking north (*see* p. 77, same viewpoint). The building on the right then housed the offices of the Yiewsley Urban District Council.

High Street, *c.* 1900. Another view of the northern end looking north towards Rabb's Corner and The Pump (*see* p. 68).

Smith & Haynes ironmongery shop, 1983. This photograph, taken shortly before the store's closure, shows the elaborate display of tools which were a distinctive feature of the shop windows. The business was established on this site in Yiewsley High Street in 1881 when the shop front was built on to an existing house. The building still survives.

Carnival at Yiewsley, late 1950s. Part of a procession photographed at the junction of Kingston Avenue and Castle Avenue.

Barge school, 1939. In 1930 the Grand Union Canal Company provided a school for the children of canal workers. It was on a barge named *Elsdale* after a benefactor of canal boatmen. The barge school is seen here, with the buildings of the railway station in the background, shortly before it was moved to Bull's Bridge, Hayes.

CHAPTER FOUR

WEST DRAYTON

Great Western Railway station, West Drayton, c. 1900. The train departing on the left is on the down main line heading towards Slough. Passengers on the platform are waiting for an early morning fast train to London. The station was then a junction for branches to Uxbridge and Staines and many passengers travelled on these lines to join the main line at West Drayton. The widely spaced tracks are a reminder that until 1892 there were additional rails to carry broad-gauge trains.

St Martin's Vicarage. The top illustration, which dates from about 1810, is of the original building. It apparently stood to the west of the road now known as Station Road and near the church. The illustration is taken from a small watercolour purchased for the church by the Revd L.E. Prout who was vicar of St Martin's from 1928 until 1956. The lower photograph, dating from 1952, is of a more recent vicarage; it stood on the opposite side of Station Road from the earlier building and further south. Its oldest part dated from the seventeenth century but there were considerable eighteenth- and nineteenth-century additions. It was acquired for use as a vicarage in 1888 and was demolished in 1962.

Station Road, view looking north near the junction with Church Road, *c.* 1900. The houses behind the trees on the right were built in 1881 and are known as De Burgh Crescent. The building on the left is the schoolhouse of West Drayton National School built in 1859. The house was demolished in 1938 to accommodate road widening but the remaining school building continued in use until 1947.

The newly completed Six Bells public house, Station Road, 1938. It replaced an old inn probably dating from the seventeenth century of the same name which stood on the same site.

Station Road, 1950s. The buildings on the left date from the early 1930s and those on the right are somewhat later.

Swan Road, c. 1900. On the right is Swain's (see p. 85) and on the left behind the wall the extensive grounds of Drayton House. This estate dated from the fifteenth century and covered the area between Swan Road and Colham Mill Road. In the late nineteenth century it was bought by W.S. Stacy and became known locally as Stacy's Park. The estate was sold in 1923, the mansion demolished and a new road constructed through the middle of the grounds; it was named Ferrers Avenue after Earl Ferrers who had owned the estate in the eighteenth century.

Elm Cottages, Swan Road, *c*. 1935. These cottages, probably dating from the sixteenth century, stood on the north side of Station Road opposite the junction with Swan Road. They are seen here just before their demolition in the 1930s as part of a slum clearance scheme.

Swain's, Swan Road, *c*. 1900. This house dates from the seventeenth century and takes its name from a local family of that period. There were additions to the building in the eighteenth and nineteenth centuries and in recent years most of the grounds have been sold for development. In 1968 the oldest part of the house was demolished to make way for road improvements.

Georgian cottages, Swan Road, 1963. These eighteenth-century houses adjacent to The Swan Inn in Swan Road are seen here shortly before they were demolished to be replaced by modern housing.

West Drayton Green, *c*. 1936. This photograph of the northern extremity of The Green about 1936 shows The Swan Inn and adjoining cottages on the left; they probably dated from the sixteenth century. On the right is the butcher's shop, at the corner of a building which was originally the West Drayton workhouse dating from the early nineteenth century. This building survives but The Swan Inn and the cottages were demolished in 1964–5.

Endsley, Church Road, 1900. This was the largest of a row of houses built in Church Road in 1881. It was occupied from that date by Uxbridge solicitor William Mercer and his family. It is seen here in 1900 decorated with flags to celebrate the relief of Mafeking. The lower photograph is a family group at Endsley about 1909. Mr and Mrs William Mercer are on the left, their daughter Lucy holds a pet monkey and on the right are their son Guy and Mr Mercer's brother, Mr John Mercer of Uxbridge. Miss Lucy Mercer continued to live at Endsley until her death in 1968. The house was demolished soon afterwards.

View of Church Lane (now known as Church Road) looking from The Green, *c.* 1900. On the left is the building which was the West Drayton workhouse until 1836. By 1900 it housed shops and was known as Prospect Place. Beyond is the sixteenth-century boundary wall of the old Manor House, incorporating the building known as The Barracks. On the right are some nineteenth-century cottages which were demolished as part of slum clearance schemes in the 1930s. On the same side of the road in the distance is Endsley (*see* p. 87).

Road widening at the junction of Station Road and Brandville Road, 1938. The buildings on the right known as The Parade were built in 1908 and still survive.

Peace celebrations, West Drayton, 1919. The First World War ended on 11 November 1918 at a time of year not conducive to outdoor activities. During the following spring and summer celebrations were held across the land. The photograph shows a procession which formed part of the celebrations at West Drayton.

Comforts Funds fête, *c.* 1942. This fête was held during the Second World War in aid of the RAF Comforts Fund on the Recreation Ground of the Power Plant Company, Kingston Lane. Such events were common during the Second World War and formed part of the 'Holidays at Home' campaign. The houses in the background are at the end of Bellclose Road.

The Green. The top photograph dates from about 1905. The buildings, from the left, are the Brewery Tap, Thatcher's Britannia Brewery, the King's Head public house, the large nineteenth-century residence Elmsdale, Swift's draper's shop and the terrace of Daisy Villas built in 1896. The view has changed little during the intervening years. The lower photograph is of The Green looking north about 1935. Through the trees can be seen Prospect Place, Britannia Works (the former brewery), Elmsdale and Daisy Villas.

Bomb damage, 1940. On the night of 15/16 November 1940, bombs were dropped around West Drayton Green and one of the buildings damaged was the presbytery of St Catherine's Roman Catholic church.

The Anglers' Retreat, *c.* 1950. This nineteenth-century riverside public house stands in Cricketfield Road near West Drayton Mill. Before it was given its present name it was known as The Anglers' Arms and The Complete Angler.

The Copse, *c.* 1920 (top) and early 1900s (bottom). This was a Tudor farmhouse which stood on the corner of West Drayton Green and Money Lane. It had been refaced in brick and an extension was added in the late eighteenth century. Until 1919 it was the home of the Batt family who were farmers in West Drayton for many generations. It later became an hotel, then a school in the 1930s and then a private house before it was demolished in 1966.

Weir Cottage, *c.* 1910. This stood between the rivers Colne and Frays close to where they rejoin and was destroyed by fire in the 1940s. In the photograph an Edwardian motor car with its proud owner is posed in Cricketfield Road with the cottage in the background.

West Drayton Mill, early 1900s. A water-mill existed at West Drayton at the time of the Domesday Survey in 1086 and in 1559 two corn mills and a malt mill were housed under the same roof. By 1696 it was largely producing paper although corn milling continued for many years. In 1796 it was acquired by Nicholas Mercer, mealman and papermaker, who rebuilt the whole complex about 1800 and by 1876 it was described as the largest millboard mill in existence – millboard is a stout pasteboard used for bookbinding etc.. In 1893 the Mercer family sold its interest in the mill to the West Drayton Millboard Co. Ltd A succession of fires occurred at the end of the nineteenth century and another in 1904 caused considerable damage. The mill finally closed after an even more serious fire in 1913 and remained derelict for many years.

West Drayton Mill. The top photograph shows the narrow roadway over the Mill Bridge. It had been a cause for concern for many years and here a group of local councillors are seen inspecting the site in 1929. More than 40 years were to elapse before any improvements were made. The lower photograph shows the Mill House in about 1900. The Mill House survived the fires and after Penguin Books Ltd acquired the site in 1947 it was converted into flats for company use.

Mill Road, *c.* 1900. View looking north towards The Green. The house was known as Copse Cottage and formed part of the estate of The Copse (*see* p. 92).

Rubbish disposal, *c.* 1935. The area to the east of Yiewsley and West Drayton, and adjacent to the canal, was extensively worked, first for brickmaking and then for gravel extraction, in the latter half of the nineteenth and early twentieth centuries. The holes left by the excavations were later filled in with domestic rubbish from London. The photograph shows barges in one of the many branches of the canal loaded with rubbish. The district was originally known as Starveall but in 1912 was renamed Stockley at the instigation of Broad & Co who owned brickworks there. The uncontrolled dumping of rubbish meant that the area became a byword for dereliction but it was successfully redeveloped in the 1980s as a business area called Stockley Park.

Aerial photograph of the West Drayton/Harmondsworth area, 1961. The railway main line and the Grand Union Canal run across the top of the photograph from east to west. Yiewsley lies mostly off the map in the top left-hand corner and in the top right-hand corner the devastation caused by the gravel workings at Stockley can be clearly seen. West Drayton occupies most of the top left-hand quadrant to the south of the railway. The southern half of the area is as yet undisturbed by the M4 motorway and its connecting roads which now disfigure the landscape. Most of this area at the time of the photograph was still in intensive agricultural use, the only breaks being the built-up areas of Harmondsworth village (in the bottom left-hand corner) and the linear village of Sipson in the middle of the bottom section of the photograph. (Photograph courtesy of Aerofilms Ltd)

CHAPTER FIVE

HARMONDSWORTH –
WITH HEATHROW,
LONGFORD & SIPSON

Greetings from Harmondsworth, c. 1910. Four of the five views depicted in this postcard have changed little since the photographs were taken. The sad exception is the view at the bottom left which shows the half-timbered Elizabethan cottages which were demolished in 1937.

Church and the Great Barn. The top view was taken from Moor Lane and shows the view of the church and barn from the west. In the foreground is the site of Harmondsworth priory which was established soon after the Norman invasion and, until 1391, came under the control of the Abbey of Holy Trinity in Rouen. Control of the manor then passed to Winchester College and the barn, which dates from about 1450, was built by the College. At 191 ft in length and 38 ft in width it is one of the largest medieval barns in England. The bottom view was taken from the M4 motorway and although quite recent (1988) could have been taken at any time in the last 150 years. It was referred to in Pevsner's *London 3: North West, The Buildings of England,* (1991) as an 'all too rare glimpse of the quiet, uneventful Middlesex countryside, with barn and church rising above the willow-lined water meadows'. It has now vanished for ever to make way for British Airways' Prospect Park development. If a third runway at Heathrow were ever to be built, and it has been seriously considered, it would go through the middle of this picture.

TO THE GLORY OF GOD
AND TO COMMEMORATE THE LOYALTY
COURAGE DEVOTION AND SELF-SACRIFICE
OF THE 417 MEN FROM THE PARISH OF
HARMONDSWORTH WHO SERVED THEIR
KING AND COUNTRY DURING THE GREAT
WAR 1914-1918 OF WHOM THE FOLLOWING
92 LAID DOWN THEIR LIVES

HARMONDSWORTH

BEARD E H		SLAYMAKER A
BENSON R C		STRATFORD A W
EDWARDS S	HOCKLEY H T	NICHOLS A J	TAYLOR S
GINGER H	HOCKLEY L C	PICKERING R H	WAKLEY A E
GINGER J	LINTILL W	PREATER G M	WAKLEY W G
GROVE H L	MARTIN E	PULLEN E	WHITE G
HARPER H J	McCOUGH J	SADLER J	WIGLESWORTH D
HATHAWAY F	MEACOCK A	SEYMOUR G J	YOUNG J R

LONGFORD

BRYANT C		RUBY A J
COWDREY E J		SESSIONS E
DU ROSE H A	DU ROSE H J	HAWKETT H E	WHITE H
	EGGLETON W	PUZEY W

HEATHROW

BURT J M		EGGLETON J
BURTON H		LIPSCOMBE G T
BURTON J	DICKENSON F G	DOWDEN J T	RUFFLE A

St SAVIOUR'S BATH RD

BUCKLAND W		MARSHALL F G
BUTLER E		MUNDY E
CARROD F A	CRIPPS F J	HOWELL A	PERRYMAN J
CONNELL A	CRIPPS G T	JONES A	SAUNDERS C D
CONNELL C	DARBON C		SEYMOUR F
CORDERY G T	EVANS S	LEWIS A J	SMITH W E
CRIPPS A T	GRAY W	LITTLE W C	WIGGINS E

SIPSON

ANDREWS J		KNIGHT E C
BUSBY E		KNIGHT O
CHANDLER J	ELDRIDGE T	LOVERIDGE A
COTTERELL R	GRAY A J	MITCHELL J R
DOPSON E H	GRAY W W	ROGERS J W
DYBLE J R	HIGGS E	SANSUM G H
TAYLOR W C	TILLEY A J	
UNDERWOOD F W	UNDERWOOD G	
WALDEN F N	WHITE W	
	WINCHCOMBE A	

THEIR NAME
LIVETH FOR
EVERMORE

Ecclus
xLiv
14

Harmondsworth War Memorial. Harmondsworth parish sent 417 men — virtually all aged between eighteen and thirty-five — to serve in the armed forces in the First World War of these ninety-two (22 per cent) were killed and many of the survivors were seriously injured. At the end of the First World War, the Parish Council decided that the War Memorial should take the form of a commemorative plaque placed inside the church and this is shown above. Each of the settlements in the parish is mentioned except for Sipson Green, better known as 'The Magpies' — after the two public houses The Three Magpies and The Old Magpies. This is recorded under the genteelism of 'St Saviour's', Bath Road — an area never heard of before or since — presumably to avoid what the church authorities would have regarded as the defilement of the church with the names of two public houses.

BRITISH   LEGION

HARMONDSWORTH BRANCH

ORDER OF SERVICE

AT THE

DEDICATION

of

TREES OF REMEMBRANCE

IN THE

WAR MEMORIAL RECREATION GROUND

SIPSON WAY   -   -   HARMONDSWORTH

On Saturday, February 9th, 1935

AT 3 p.m.

ADDRESS BY

Rev. DAVID RAILTON, M.C.

Dedication of the War Memorial Recreation Ground, 1935. As well as placing the plaque inside the church, the Parish Council decided subscriptions should be invited to raise enough money to buy a piece of land as a War Memorial Recreation Ground. The first site chosen for the recreation ground was on the Bath Road adjoining Sipson and Heathrow school and opposite The Old Magpies (*see* p. 124). This site was not ideal and in 1930, when Blunts Field on the north-west corner of the Bath Road and Sipson Way came on the market, it was decided to purchase this land as a replacement. As Blunts Field was far larger than the former site, council houses (now Blunts Avenue) were built on the southern part of the field and only the northern portion was laid out as a recreation ground with an entrance from Sipson Way. It was dedicated at a ceremony on 9 February 1935 when trees were planted in memory of those killed in the war. Sadly none of these trees survive; some died from natural causes, some from casual vandalism but most from mass vandalism on the part of the Yiewsley and West Drayton Urban District Council which removed all the trees from the recreation ground in the early 1960s.

British Legion parade, 1936. The photograph shows members of the Harmondsworth branch of the British Legion marching through the village on Sunday 14 June 1936. The parade, headed by the Yiewsley and West Drayton Silver Band, was on its way to the church for the dedication of the standard of the women's branch. In spite of this, the women brought up the rear of the parade and cannot be seen in the photograph! Similar parades were held annually in November on Remembrance Sunday. The row of cottages in the background is Blacksmith's Row which was demolished in 1937. (Photograph courtesy of *Uxbridge Gazette* newspapers)

The Harmondsworth fire engine. A second-hand fire engine was acquired by Harmondsworth Parish Council in 1879 and still exists. On one side appears the date 1879 and on the other 1905, the year in which it was renovated. Until it was replaced, it was stored in an engine shed in Moor Lane just past the Five Bells. With the changes in local government administration, the engine passed from the ownership of the Parish Council to the Yiewsley and West Drayton Urban District Council and then to Hillingdon Borough Council. It remains within the borough but is now in private ownership.

Members of the Harmondsworth Volunteer Fire Brigade, 1930. The four firemen are the Chief Officer, Samuel Bateman (seated), and standing behind him, left to right, are his three sons – Eric, Hubert and William. Samuel Bateman (1858–1937) had a remarkable record in the fire brigade. He joined as a 'call-out boy' and served in various ranks for sixty-eight years, thirty-six of which as Chief Officer. Following the reorganisation of local government in 1930, responsibility for the fire service passed to the Yiewsley and West Drayton urban district council. This may be the reason for the photograph which was taken in June 1930.

Manor Farm, 1967. At the time that this photograph was taken this was a working farm and the fifteenth-century Great Barn, which is part of the Manor Farm complex, was still in agricultural use as it had been for the previous 500 years. Soon after, permission was given for the farmhouse to be converted to office accommodation in return for the restoration of the Great Barn and the surrounding area. The conversion and restoration have been tastefully done with no harm to the historic centre of the village. The farmhouse dates from the early nineteenth century and is believed to occupy the site of the former manor house.

Sun House, 1967. Although much altered, this is the oldest residential property in the village, dating from the sixteenth century. Under the external brick cladding it is half-timbered and still retains the main timber frame, now concealed within the later brickwork. In 1586 it was granted by Queen Elizabeth I in trust for the 'perpetual maintenance of lights, lamps and so forth in the church of Harmondsworth'. It remained in the ownership of the church until quite recently. It was a public house (The Sun) until 1912 and a butcher's shop until much later. Because of its proximity to the church it was regularly used by the churchwardens and Parish Council to hold meetings.

The Grange, Summerhouse Lane, 1976. This is the view from the south (garden side) of the house; the front is difficult to see because of the high wall which originally ran for the whole length of Summerhouse Lane. The age of the building is pinpointed by the date 1675 which appears in a sunken brick panel over the doorway. It is a handsome red-brick building typical of the period and inside is a very fine original staircase. Between the sash windows on the upper storey shown there was once a painted wooden sun dial which bore the date 1695; it was sold for £1 7s 6d at an auction in May 1937. In the 1950s the house became dilapidated and was well restored in the 1970s as office accommodation.

Harmondsworth Hall, Summerhouse Lane. This house stands almost opposite The Grange from which this photograph was taken. It is probably older than its neighbour, although the exterior and fine Georgian doorway might suggest otherwise because they were both remodelled in the eighteenth century. Up until about thirty years ago the gardens of the hall and those of The Grange ran for the length of Summerhouse Lane with a high wall on either side of the lane. The present-day housing estates in the lane were built in the grounds of the two houses.

Harmondsworth Vicarage, top *c.* 1910, bottom 1966. When the earlier photograph was taken the whole of this large building was used as the vicarage by the Revd John Taylor. The people standing outside are presumably members of his family with their servants. By 1966 the building had been divided into three residential units with only the part nearest the church being used by the vicar. Since then a completely new vicarage has been built between the former vicarage and the church. The old building has been renamed Tower House and is now used as a nursery. A vicarage had existed on the site since the early fifteenth century but the building shown in the photograph dates from 1845 with later additions including the tower at the eastern end. To the right of the vicarage, in the lower photograph, is the former vicarage hall which was opened in 1885 and demolished in 1972.

Cherry orchard, Hatch Lane, 1969. Rocque's map of Middlesex, published in 1754, shows an orchard on this site so the land must have been used for fruit growing for more than 200 years. It was the last sizeable orchard in the district but was grubbed up soon after this photograph was taken. At the turn of the twentieth century fruit growing was one of the most important industries of West Middlesex; in 1900 almost one-third of the land in Harmondsworth parish was covered with orchards. This led Stephen Springall, in his *Country Rambles around Uxbridge* (1907), to comment 'Fruit trees we shall find to obtain in this neighbourhood for all round Harmondsworth, Harlington, Sipson and Heathrow are thousands of fruit trees which flourish in perfection in the flat and open country.'

Grave of Richard Cox, Harmondsworth Churchyard. The Cox's Orange Pippin apple began life in the garden of Richard Cox who lived on the Middlesex side of Colnbrook. In 1830 Cox planted two pips of a Ribston Pippin, one of which germinated into the variety which now bears his name. The tree was passed to Messrs R. Small of Slough in 1836 and put on the market four years later. Since then it has remained the best-known variety of English apple. Cox's wife Ann died on 9 February 1837 and Richard eight years later on 20 May 1845, when he was seventy-nine. In his will he expressed a desire 'to be buried in the same grave as my dear wife in the churchyard of the parish of Harmondsworth'. The grave is still there, well built and preserved, standing under a yew tree close to the north-east corner of the church.

H.C. Belch and Sons, builders and stonemasons, *c*. 1910. The firm's premises stood on the north side of the junction of Hatch Lane, Holloway Lane and the village High Street. This photograph shows Henry Carey Belch (1843–1934) on the right with his youngest son Fred (1873–1949).As well as running his business H.C. Belch was, at different times, chairman of Staines Rural District Council, captain of the volunteer fire brigade, clerk to both the burial board and the fire service and an active supporter of the local Baptist churches. Soon after his death the premises were taken over by F.A. James, a local coal merchant. The site was renamed the Central Garage by its next owner W. Hicks and remained in use for car repairs and petrol sales until the 1970s. The front of the building shown in the photograph was demolished in the early 1990s but the back, which can be seen below, remains.

Baptist church and Central Garage, 1967. The Baptists have had a church in the village since at least 1833 when Harlington Baptist church, founded in 1798 (*see* p. 53), started to extend its influence to the surrounding villages. The original chapel, which occupied a site on the other side of the High Street, was destroyed by fire in 1884. The present building on the corner of Hatch Lane and the High Street took its place. To the right of the church is the Central Garage which began life as the premises of H.C. Belch and Sons.

The new Peggy Bedford, Colnbrook bypass. This local landmark occupied a prominent position at the junction of the Colnbrook bypass and the Old Bath Road for almost seventy years. To the residents of Harmondsworth, and no doubt travellers using the Bath Road (A4), its demolition in September 1995 seemed an unnecessary act of vandalism. Had it been a few yards further down either road it would probably have been spared, but because of its prominent position it was decided that a replacement petrol station and a drive-in takeaway would be more profitable. The top photograph was taken in the early 1930s from the Colnbrook bypass soon after the hotel opened. The lower photograph was taken outside the hotel in 1953 soon after the coronation. The spectators are waiting for Queen Elizabeth and the Duke of Edinburgh to drive by on their way to Windsor.

Coronation celebrations, 1937. This photograph was taken soon after the coronation of King George VI, on 12 May 1937. The crowd is waiting for the King and Queen to drive by on their way to Windsor; their car can just be seen in the middle of the picture. The scene took place on the Old Bath Road outside the new Peggy Bedford which is out of view to the left. The houses in the background are in Hatch Lane; they are still there but can no longer be seen from this vantage point. First to obscure the view was the Black & Decker factory (below) then much later came the Sheraton Hotel and Summit Centre. A hideous airport multi-storey car park now stands behind where the crowd appears on the extreme right of the photograph.

Black & Decker Ltd, Bath Road, 1967. The opening of the Colnbrook bypass in 1929 was followed quickly by ribbon industrial development along the Bath Road. Black & Decker Ltd was the last major firm to settle in the parish before the construction of Heathrow Airport. The factory, at the junction of the Bath Road with Hatch Lane, opened in 1940 and by 1960 it had 1,100 employees making portable electric tools. Unfortunately, like so many other industries in the vicinity of Heathrow, the firm found it more profitable to sell the site and to relocate to an area where land values were lower. The factory was demolished in the early 1980s and the site is now occupied by an industrial estate known as Summit Centre.

Rear view of The Stables, formerly the old Peggy Bedford, Longford. The old Peggy Bedford formerly known as the King's Head stood on the Old Bath Road about 800 yd west of the now demolished hotel of the same name (*see* p. 108). The licence was transferred to the new premises in 1928 when the Colnbrook bypass was built and this building became a private house. On 22 January 1934 the front was completely destroyed by fire but the rear was relatively undamaged and, with its rebuilt front, is now a private house known as The Stables. Next to the house are some half-timbered mock-Tudor modern houses one of which, Phoenix House, was built from salvaged materials from the old Peggy Bedford – hence the name.

Yeomans, Longford, 1954. There is no question about the authenticity of this building which is a genuine sixteenth-century timber-framed house. It remains in good condition and is little changed in appearance from this photograph.

Weekly House, Longford, 1939. The Weekly family, from which this house derives its name, first appears in the parish records in 1688. The last member of the family with that name to live in the house was Richard who died in 1875. On the death of his widow, in 1898, the house passed to H.J. Wild who was closely related to the family. His eldest son William was living here at the time this photograph was taken. The house, which dates from the late seventeenth century, was damaged on 15 June 1944 by one of the first V-1 flying bombs to fall in Britain. It was renovated after the war but by the 1980s had again fallen into disrepair and was restored to provide office accommodation.

Blacksmith's shop, Longford, c. 1912. This photograph was taken outside the wheelwright's shop (on the left) and forge (on the right) of T.W. Adams the village blacksmith and wheelwright. The larger than life character is Henry James Wild (1831–1915) and his mode of dress belongs to the period of his youth some sixty years earlier; he had taken a horse plough into the village forge to be repaired. The other two people are Thomas Adams, the blacksmith, facing the camera and his assistant. H.J. Wild was the founder of the farming business H.J.Wild and Sons and his farm was next to Weekly House, only a short distance away from the forge.

King's Bridge, Longford. The top photograph, which dates from about 1910, shows the view from King's Bridge looking in an easterly direction. Florence Villas, since demolished, are on the right-hand side of the road with The King's Arms at the far end of the villas; on the left in the distance is the roof of Weekly House. The bottom photograph was taken in 1969 and shows the southern side of the bridge. Since then the monogram, seen in the photograph, has been stolen but similar monograms on the road sides of the bridge are still in place. The present bridge was built in the reign of King William IV, as can be seen from the monogram which bears the inscription 'W.IV.R. 1834'. It derives its name from the fact that the Crown is responsible for its upkeep. The river which it bridges is an artificial channel cut in the reign of Charles I (1625–49) to improve the water supply to Hampton Court. It has various names but for most of its route it is known as the Longford River. The river leaves the Colne, about half a mile north of the bridge, and originally flowed in a southerly direction as far as Stanwell before turning south-east to Hampton Court. Its course was changed in the 1940s as a result of the construction of Heathrow Airport so that at one point it now goes underground and shares a channel with the Duke of Northumberland's River.

Sipson Road, 1906. The cart-load of cabbages has been horse-drawn to the field entrance and is being hitched to the steam wagon to take it back to the farmyard. The steam engine, which also features in a later photograph (*see* p. 122), has 'Perseverance 1903' written on its side. R.R. Robbins, co-partner of Wild and Robbins, watches the proceedings from his bicycle. Tom Mullins, the carter watches from the other side while Alf Chandler, the engine driver, is manoeuvring the engine into position. It would probably have been quicker to dispense with the steam engine and to have allowed the cart to be horse-drawn all the way to the farmyard which was less than half a mile away. The cart is coming out of the field gate seen on the left of the picture below.

Sipson Road after a blizzard, 1952. This view was taken from the same point as the previous photograph and shows the scene in Sipson Road between West Drayton and Sipson after a freak weekend blizzard in March 1952. Snow had been blown off the fields on either side of the road and then trapped by the hedges. The road remained blocked for several days and traffic between Sipson and West Drayton had to go via Harmondsworth. The silhouettes of the buildings in the north of Sipson village can be seen in the distant gloom. On the left is The Plough and to its right are Vinery Cottages which were demolished in the early 1960s. The field on the left is now the site of the Forte Crest (formerly Post House) Hotel; the field gate is approximately where the entrance of the hotel now stands.

Sipson village, north end. Both of these views show Sipson Road leading into Sipson from the direction of West Drayton. The top photograph taken in the 1920s shows, on the extreme right, The Welcome coffee tavern which was built in 1897 as a counter-attraction to the three public houses in the village. To the left is Centre House, which was a butcher's shop and dated from the early nineteenth century. In the centre of the photograph is the King William which dates from the sixteenth century. Although disguised by re-fronting, this is an unusual example, for Middlesex, of a Wealden-type medieval hall house. To the left are some seventeenth-century cottages which were demolished in the 1930s. The lower photograph taken in 1969 is almost the same view with the buildings of Sipson Farm on the left. These two views show how the King William was re-fronted in the early 1930s. It is the only building of those featured which still remains.

Sipson village centre, *c.* 1910. The top photograph was taken from a point in Sipson Road about 200 yd south of the previous illustrations and looking in the opposite direction. In the far distance is The Welcome coffee tavern and in front of this is Centre House, which was Appleton's baker's at the time this photograph was taken. Later it became a butcher's shop. The houses in the middle stood next to the King William and were pulled down in the early 1930s. The houses on the left (now nos 406 to 408 Sipson Road) are the only buildings which still remain. The bottom photograph was taken from the same position but looking in the opposite direction. Appleton's Cottages, which stretched round the corner into Sipson Lane, are on the left. On the right is Hollycroft partially obscured by its garden wall and trees. In the far distance is Gladstone Terrace.

Sipson village store and post office, 1970. The back portion of the village store and post office is half-timbered and is probably the oldest building in Sipson. The front, which faces the road, is a Victorian addition. It has been the village store since at least the mid-nineteenth century. In 1832 it was sold by Thomas Everingham, 'a shopkeeper, late of Sipson', to James Starnes, 'a grocer of Sipson', for the sum of £250. The shop remained in the Starnes family for the remainder of the nineteenth century.

Sipson village, southern end, c. 1920. Except for the house on the extreme left, most of the buildings in this picture remain. To the right of this house are Holly Cottages, now 432 to 450 Sipson Road, built in 1906 and named after Hollycroft, the home of R.R. Robbins. On the extreme right of the picture is part of Gladstone Terrace, a block of five houses built in the 1880s and now renumbered 415 to 423 Sipson Road. In the middle distance is The Crown public house.

Sipson Farmhouse, *c.* 1905. Members of the Wild family have lived in the parish since at least the mid-1600s. Their main residence was the old seventeenth-century farmhouse shown in this photograph. The side wall of The Vineries (*see* below) can be seen to the right of the house and the gate on the left led into the yard of Sipson Farm. R.R. Robbins, the junior partner of Wild and Robbins, lived in The Vineries when it was vacated by Thomas Wild. His son Lionel – Lord Robbins, the education reformer – was born here in 1898. The house was demolished shortly after the photograph was taken.

The Vineries, Sipson Road, *c.* 1905. The photograph shows the rear of the late Victorian house which was built for Thomas Wild I (1848–1932). On the extreme right of the photograph Sipson Farm (Wild's previous house) can just be seen. The other building in the photograph is The Welcome coffee tavern which stood opposite The Vineries and was built in a very similar style. The house was demolished in 1970 and the site is now occupied by homes in Vineries Close.

Hollycroft, Sipson Road, *c.* 1935. This is the late Georgian house which stood next to the village stores (*see* p. 116). From 1904 until the early 1950s it was the home of R.R. Robbins; it was sold by him to a local doctor and was later used by an airport catering firm. It was demolished in the late 1960s and the site is occupied by the houses in Hollycroft Close.

Inglenook, Sipson Lane, *c.* 1910. This house was built for Thomas Wild II (1879–1965) at the time of his marriage to Elizabeth Rayner. On the death of his father, Thomas moved to The Vineries and his son Thomas Wild III (1907–55) became the occupant. The house was sold by the family in the 1980s and is now used as the Buffer Bear Day Nursery. To the left are some of the glasshouses of Sipson Farm and above these the roof of The Vineries can just be seen.

The Gables, Sipson Road, 1969. This house was built in 1907 by Portsmouth's of Harlington for the occupation of Arthur Philp of Sipson on his marriage to Eliza Philp of Harlington – the marriage brought together the Sipson and Harlington branches of the family after an interval of five generations. The house was extended about 1930 and demolished in the early 1970s. Numbers 459 to 463 Sipson Road now occupy the site.

Milk delivery by handcart, 1940s. The photograph shows Mrs Stroud, who worked for Clifford's Dairies, delivering milk in Blunts Avenue, Sipson. Pushing a handcart fully laden with milk bottles was very hard work and was only feasible for short distances. Clifford's Dairies of Hounslow had a local branch on the Bath Road only half a mile away. One of their milkmen, who was rather short, was known locally as 'Flat-out' on account of the almost horizontal position he had to adopt to push his handcart. Milk deliveries over longer distances were traditionally done by horse-drawn carts but by the mid-1930s electric-powered milk floats were introduced by the larger dairies.

'Whittington's' Farm, Harmondsworth Lane, Sipson, 1939. This eighteenth-century farmhouse is one of the only two listed buildings now remaining in Sipson. It has never had a permanent name but always seems to have taken its name from the owner at the time. Hence in the sale details of 1898, which are printed below, it was known as Whittington's Farm. It was sold by Richard Whittington in 1919 to Henry Trusler whereupon it became known as Trusler's Farm and is now known as Lanz Farm. The house has changed little since 1898 and the description given in the sales brochure still applies.

LOT TWO (*Coloured Blue on Plan*).

COMPRISES AN EXCELLENT COMPACT

FREEHOLD PROPERTY

KNOWN AS

"Whittington's Farm,"

Situate at SIPSON in the PARISH OF HARMONDSWORTH,

Between Harmondsworth and Harlington, and about 2 Miles from West Drayton Station (G.W.R.)

COMPRISING A BRICK AND SLATED AND TILED

DETACHED DWELLING HOUSE

CONTAINING

Three Bedrooms	Two Living Rooms	Coal House, and
Box Room	Kitchen, Larder	Outside W.C.

THERE ARE

EXCELLENT FARM BUILDINGS

WHICH COMPRISE

A large Timber and Tiled Cart Shed with Lean-to Brick and Tiled Stables for 3 Horses each;
Large Slated Barn, and 2 Lean-to's.

Potato planting, Whittington's Farm, *c.* 1912. Potato planting with hand dibbers may be acceptable in a garden but even at the time this photograph was taken it would have been unusual to see it being done on a large scale. The field where the men are standing is just to the west of the farmhouse (*see* p. 120). The houses in the background, which were demolished in the early 1960s, stood in Harmondsworth Lane. The house on the left was approximately where the entrance to Heathrow School is now situated. The two men with dibbers are believed to be Albert (Mick) Whittington on the left and his older brother Richard.

Riddling potatoes, Sipson Farm, *c.* 1950. Grading potatoes at this time was still labour-intensive. The machine for doing the task was known as a riddle which was like a large sieve and required three men for its operation. The man at the rear shovelled potatoes onto the vibrating riddle. The smaller potatoes fell through the holes in the riddle and were sold separately as animal feed. The man in the middle then examined those remaining and removed any that were damaged or diseased. Those that survived the sorting process were then fed into sacks held by the third man.

Plough teams at Sipson Farm, *c.* 1910. The top photograph shows a four-horse plough team at work in the fields between Sipson Road and Holloway Lane along the line of what is now the M4 motorway. Horse-drawn ploughs were the main form of cultivation and were still used for small-scale work as late as 1950. Wild and Robbins also owned steam engines that were sometimes used for ploughing. The bottom photograph shows one of these in use but they could only be used in dry weather because the wheels soon sank into wet soil. Judging from the photographs, steam ploughing was just as labour-intensive as horse ploughing. The steam engine (*see also* p. 113) bears the inscription 'Perseverance 1903'.

Preparing for market, Sipson Farm, *c.* 1905. Vegetables bound for Covent Garden market were prepared in the packing shed and placed in bushel baskets made from locally grown willows. These were loaded on to carts which were either drawn by horses or, as in this case, by a steam traction-engine. The carts did not return empty: instead one would bring back the baskets from two cart-loads of vegetables; the other would be loaded with manure from the London stables to be used as a valuable fertiliser on the farm. Without this means of waste disposal London, with its huge number of horse-drawn vehicles, would have soon been buried in horse manure. The engine in the photograph bears the name and date 'Pioneer 1902'. The building on the extreme left is The Welcome coffee tavern.

Box making, Sipson Farm, *c.* 1910. Being circular, the bushel baskets seen in the top photograph left a lot of empty space on the carts. Rectangular boxes stacked much better but offered little advantage over round baskets because although more could be loaded on the carts, the vehicles then became too heavy to be drawn by the horses. As horses were replaced by traction-engines, greater weights could be hauled and the baskets therefore gradually gave way to boxes. Wild and Robbins were nothing if not self-sufficient: as can be seen in this photograph, they even made their own boxes.

Recreation ground and St Saviour's church, Bath Road. Before it was moved to its present location in Sipson Way (*see* p. 100), the Harmondsworth War Memorial Recreation Ground occupied a site on the north side of the Bath Road between Sipson and Heathrow School and St Saviour's church. The upper photograph, taken in 1931 flatters the church but whether or not it flatters the boy is not for the author to say. The church was nothing more than a corrugated iron structure, known locally as the Tin Church, which was built in 1880 to serve this part of Harmondsworth parish. It was demolished in 1934 and replaced with the brick building shown in the lower photograph. This picture, taken in 1943, shows the curate Revd Albert Croft with his Model Y Ford 8 which has visors over its headlamps to comply with wartime blackout regulations. The building was intended to be the church hall to a new church which was never built. In the early 1960s the Excelsior Hotel and the M4/Airport Spur Road were built on the site, and the spot where the boy is standing is now occupied by a large roundabout.

Preparation of Fairey's airfield for grass sowing, 1930. In 1929 the Fairey Aviation Company of Hayes bought some 200 acres of land at Heathrow for use as an airfield for its trial flights. The fields purchased by the company were levelled and laid out as an area of high quality turf and used as an airfield for the first time in late 1930. This photograph shows the preparatory work for the turfing. The aircraft hangar is in the background. In 1944 Fairey's airfield was requisitioned by the Air Ministry, under the pretext that it was needed for military purposes, to become the nucleus of Heathrow Airport.

Model aircraft flying, Heathrow, 1930s. Richard Fairey started his career by selling model aeroplanes. Because of his youthful interest he was therefore very sympathetic to the requests of model aeroplane clubs to use his aerodrome at weekends when it was not being used for any other purposes. The aerodrome was the regular Sunday venue for members of the Hayes Model Aeroplane Club and this photograph was taken at one of its meetings.

Fairey Aerodrome, Heathrow, 1932. This is a view looking across to the south-west and shows that, except for the large hangar on its north-east corner, the airfield was virtually indistinguishable from the farm land which surrounded it. The road crossing the middle of the photograph in front of the hangar is Cain's Lane. What appears to be a road cutting diagonally across the photograph from the bottom right-hand edge is, in fact, nothing more than a farm track. The hamlet of Heathrow, straggling along Heathrow Road, can be seen in the top right-hand corner. (Photograph courtesy of Aerofilms Ltd)

INDEX

ACKNOWLEDGEMENTS

Except where otherwise stated, all the photographs are from negatives or originals owned by the Hayes and Harlington Local History Society, the West Drayton and District Local History Society or the private collections of P.T. Sherwood, D.M. Rust, K.R. Pearce and the late J. Hammond. Grateful thanks are due, however, to the various individuals who have donated or loaned for copying the original photographs, postcards and paintings which have been reproduced here.

These include Mrs M. Johnson • Mrs N. Lee • Mrs J. Read and Mr J. Allport Mr J. Chinery • Mr D. Francombe • Mr J. Hearne • Mr S.J. Heyward • Mr B. Hodges Mr D. Mead • Mr R. Robbins • Mr G. Stevens • Mr P. Tarrant • Mr W. Wild.